STUNNING NFL UPSETS
12 SHOCKERS FROM NFL HISTORY

by Matt Scheff

12 STORY LIBRARY

www.12StoryLibrary.com

Copyright © 2016 by Peterson Publishing Company, North Mankato, MN 56003. All rights reserved. No part of this book may be reproduced or utilized in any form or by any means without written permission from the publisher.

12-Story Library is an imprint of Peterson Publishing Company and Press Room Editions.

Produced for 12-Story Library by Red Line Editorial

Photographs ©: Gene Puskar/AP Images, cover, 1, 27; Pro Football Hall of Fame/AP Images, 4, 5; Pro Football Hall of Fame/NFL Photos/AP Images, 6; Bettmann/Corbis, 8; NFL Photos/AP Images, 11, 12, 15, 28; Al Golub/AP Images, 16; Bill Waugh/AP Images, 18, 29; Phil Sandlin/AP Images, 19; Michael S. Green/AP Images, 21; Elaine Thompson/AP Images, 22; Tom DiPace/AP Images, 24; Kathy Willens/AP Images, 25; Paul Spinelli/AP Images, 26

ISBN
978-1-63235-153-1 (hardcover)
978-1-63235-193-7 (paperback)
978-1-62143-245-6 (hosted ebook)

Library of Congress Control Number: 2015934298

Printed in the United States of America
Mankato, MN
June, 2015

Go beyond the book. Get free, up-to-date content on this topic at 12StoryLibrary.com.

TABLE OF CONTENTS

GIANTS SNEAK A CHAMPIONSHIP

The 1934 Chicago Bears appeared to be an unstoppable force. They had won the previous two National Football League (NFL) titles. Then they went 13–0 in 1934. The Bears won their games by an average of more than 15 points. The New York Giants, meanwhile, had often struggled. They posted a modest record of 8–5. Few expected much when the teams met for the 1934 NFL title.

December 9, 1934, was bitterly cold at the Polo Grounds in New York City. In the first half, both teams struggled to find footing on the hard, icy field. Yet the Bears controlled the action. They took a 10–3 lead into halftime.

New York Giants players tackle Chicago Bears fullback Bronko Nagurski during the 1934 NFL Championship Game.

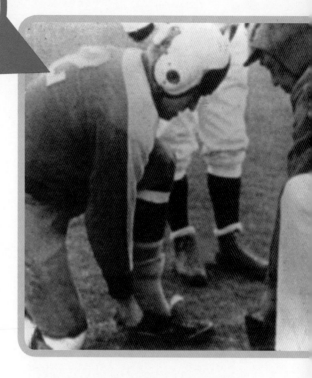

The Giants were in trouble. But team captain Ray Flaherty had an idea. The Giants' cleats were not sticking into the frozen ground. So Flaherty sent an assistant to Manhattan College to collect as many rubber-soled basketball sneakers as he could get. It was a stroke of genius. The Bears continued to slip and slide all over the field with their cleats. With their basketball shoes, the Giants were surefooted. They ran circles around the heavily favored Bears.

The rout started with a 28-yard touchdown pass from quarterback Ed Danowski to Ike Frankian. Soon after, running back Ken Strong gashed the Bears' defense with a 42-yard touchdown run. The Giants went on to outscore the Bears 27–3 in the second half. The final score was of 30–13. The game was perhaps the biggest upset in the NFL's young history. The Bears and Giants all agreed—the difference in the game was the sneakers.

18
Consecutive games the Bears had won entering the 1934 NFL Championship.

- The NFL began in 1920. However, there was no championship game until 1933.
- Ken Strong was the star of the title game for New York. The running back rushed for 94 yards and two touchdowns.

CLEVELAND MAKES A BIG SPLASH

Cleveland Browns running back Marion Motley runs with the ball during the 1950 game against the Eagles.

448

Cleveland's total offensive yards in the game. The Eagles managed just 248.

- The Browns were no fluke. They went on to win the 1950 NFL championship.
- Cleveland beat the Los Angeles Rams 30–28 in the NFL Championship Game.
- The Browns reached all but one NFL title game from 1950 to 1957. They won three times.

The Super Bowl began after the 1966 season as a game between the champions of two different leagues. Some people say the NFL's first Super Bowl actually took place on September 16, 1950. The game featured two defending champions. On the home side were the Philadelphia Eagles. They were the two-time defending NFL champs. The opposing Cleveland Browns had dominated the short-lived All-America Football Conference (AAFC). They won four titles in a row from 1946 to 1949. Then the AAFC folded. The Browns joined the NFL. And in their first game in 1950, they played the Eagles.

Despite Cleveland's success, few gave the Browns a chance. Many considered the AAFC to be a minor league. Still, a record crowd of 71,237 turned out to see the game. Most of them were Eagles fans. Most expected a rout. And that's just what they got. Only the rout wasn't quite the way they'd imagined. The Browns introduced themselves to the league by dominating the defending champs. Quarterback Otto Graham passed for 346 yards and three touchdowns. The Browns' defense was dominant, too. By the time the game was over, Eagles players and fans looked on in disbelief. Browns 35, Eagles 10.

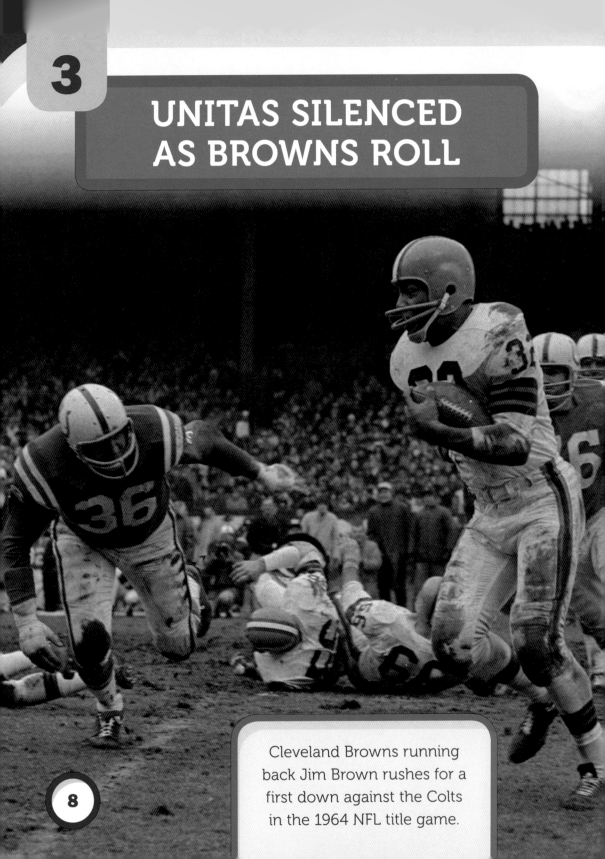

UNITAS SILENCED AS BROWNS ROLL

Cleveland Browns running back Jim Brown rushes for a first down against the Colts in the 1964 NFL title game.

The Cleveland Browns were the underdogs in the 1964 NFL Championship Game. Most fans expected star quarterback Johnny Unitas and the Baltimore Colts to win it all. Unitas led a dazzling Baltimore passing attack. Cleveland countered with a rough-and-tough running game. Powerful running back Jim Brown led the way.

Almost all of the experts predicted a Colts victory. The editors at *Sports Illustrated* were especially confident. They'd already prepared their magazine. It featured Unitas and Colts coach Don Shula on the cover.

Yet by kickoff, conditions favored the Browns' physical style. The temperature at Cleveland Municipal Stadium was below freezing. Wind gusted to 25 miles per hour (40 km/h). The cold and wind made passing difficult. Neither offense could move the ball in a scoreless first half. Then in the second half, the Browns began to roll. Brown carried the load. He rushed 27 times for 114 yards in the game. Quarterback Frank Ryan did the rest. Three times, Ryan connected with receiver Gary Collins on touchdown passes. One was a 51-yard strike that put the Browns up 27–0.

Unitas and the Colts were helpless against a stout Cleveland defense, and that score held up. The Browns walked off winners. Meanwhile, the editors of *Sports Illustrated* were left scrambling to change their cover.

0

Points scored in the first half.

- Johnny Unitas was limited to just 95 passing yards in the game.
- Cleveland also intercepted the future hall of famer Unitas two times.
- The Browns won their fourth NFL championship. It marked the last major sports title for a Cleveland team through 2014.

4

NAMATH DELIVERS ON HIS GUARANTEE

The 1968 season was a time of change in the NFL. A rival league called the American Football League (AFL) had begun play in 1960. The two leagues decided to merge. The long process began in 1966. For the next four seasons, each league still named a champion. But then their champions played each other. The game became known as the Super Bowl.

The NFL champ had dominated the first two Super Bowls. Almost everyone expected the same in Super Bowl III in January 1969. Oddsmakers listed the Baltimore Colts as an overwhelming 18-point favorite over the AFL's New York Jets.

The Jets were led by brash young quarterback Joe Namath. Three days before the big game, Namath made

headlines. In response to a heckling fan, Namath made a promise for the ages.

"We're gonna win the game," he said. "I guarantee it."

Namath had made the guarantee. But the New York defense backed it up. The Colts' offense struggled badly all game. In the second quarter, Namath led an 80-yard

4
Interceptions by the New York defense in Super Bowl III.

- Super Bowl III was the first to officially carry the name "Super Bowl."
- Joe Namath was named Super Bowl Most Valuable Player (MVP).
- However, Namath threw for just 206 yards and no touchdowns.

Joe Namath signals that his New York Jets are number one after they won Super Bowl III.

scoring drive. Running back Matt Snell finished it off with a touchdown. The score marked the AFL's first lead in any Super Bowl.

The Jets tacked on two field goals in the third quarter. Then they added another in the fourth. Fans looked on in shock as New York led 16–0. A late Baltimore touchdown ruined the shutout. But the message was clear in the Jets' 16–7 win. The AFL was finally ready to compete. And Joe Namath had forever sealed his place in Super Bowl lore.

AFL MAKES IT TWO IN A ROW

The AFL's New York Jets won in Super Bowl III. Yet that did little to raise people's opinions of the AFL. The NFL was still the better league, they argued. And the NFL champion Minnesota Vikings were heavy favorites in Super Bowl IV in January 1970. Oddsmakers listed them as 13-point favorites to beat the AFL champion Kansas City Chiefs.

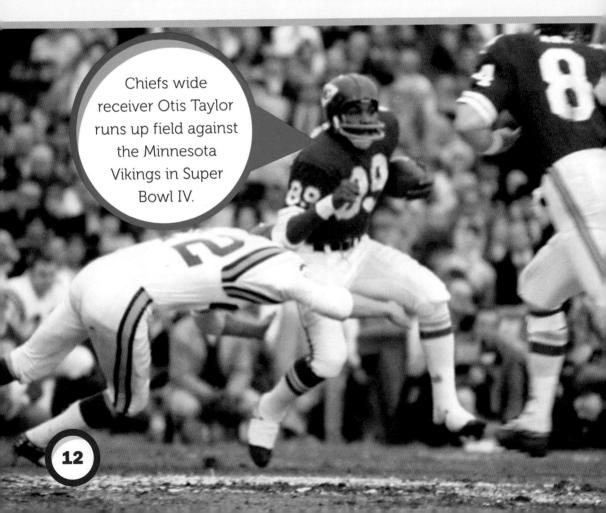

Chiefs wide receiver Otis Taylor runs up field against the Minnesota Vikings in Super Bowl IV.

The Vikings had dominated the NFL on both sides of the ball. They were best known for a fierce defensive line. It was known as "The Purple People Eaters." The Chiefs, meanwhile, had struggled just to make the playoffs before getting hot.

Yet the underdog Chiefs then made easy work of the Vikings. Their defensive line shut down Minnesota's scrambling passer, Joe Kapp. Meanwhile, running back Mike Garrett and the Chiefs gashed the Vikings defense. The Vikings managed just a single touchdown.

- Kansas City kicker Jan Stenerud made field goals of 43, 32, and 25 yards, all in the first half.
- The Vikings would go on to make three more Super Bowl appearances in the 1970s. They lost all of them.

Kansas City won 23–7. The final score provided fans with the second straight Super Bowl shocker. It also proved that the AFL was no fluke.

THE MERGER

The NFL and AFL finally completed their merger in 1970. It was a move four years in the making. The rival leagues had first agreed to merge in 1966. For four seasons, they kept separate schedules and crowned separate champions. Each champion then represented its league in the Super Bowl. Super Bowl IV marked the end of this era. The following season, the merger was official. The league split into the American Football Conference (AFC) and the National Football Conference (NFC).

THE BEARS CAN'T REPEAT

The 1985 Chicago Bears were one of the most storied teams in NFL history. They had it all. They had a crushing defense. They had a hall-of-fame running back in Walter Payton. And they had a super-cool quarterback in Jim McMahon. They were fan favorites. And they were a terror on the field. Many fans and experts expected a repeat in 1986.

The Bears rolled through the regular season at 14–2. All was not well in Chicago, though. McMahon had missed much of the season with injuries. The team couldn't settle on a replacement. Finally, coach Mike Ditka picked untested Doug Flutie. He started against the Washington Redskins in the playoffs. The move surprised many fans and media

members, and even some of the Bears players.

Ditka's choice looked like the right one when Chicago built a 13–7 lead at halftime. Everything changed in the second half. Washington quarterback Jay Schroeder hit wide receiver Art Monk with a 23-yard touchdown pass. That put Washington in the lead. Schroeder and company went on to score 20 unanswered points. Meanwhile, Flutie and the Bears couldn't get anything going. A shocked Soldier Field crowd could only watch. The 1986 Bears, favored by most to win it all, had been bounced from the playoffs 27–13. It was one of the most shocking playoff upsets in NFL history.

29–3

The Bears' combined regular-season record for 1985 and 1986.

- Chicago was listed as 7-point favorites for the Washington game.
- Washington went on to lose the NFC Championship Game to the New York Giants.

THINK ABOUT IT

Some fans think the 1986 Bears were victims of their own success. The fans didn't believe the team was as hungry to win again. Could success be an obstacle to further success? Would giving your all be harder after you've reached a championship level?

Running back Walter Payton sits in disbelief after the Chicago Bears lost to Washington.

7
VIKINGS PULL OFF BACK-TO-BACK STUNNERS

The 1987 Minnesota Vikings had barely made the playoffs at 8–7. Then they shocked everyone by beating the New Orleans Saints 44–10 in the first round. The Saints had gone 12–3. Minnesota's win looked like the upset of the year.

Minnesota Vikings linebacker Chris Doleman celebrates after a sack against the San Francisco 49ers.

But the Vikings had even more up their sleeves. They traveled to San Francisco in the divisional round. The 49ers had gone 13–2. They were one of the NFL's best teams. Future hall of famers such as Joe Montana, Jerry Rice, and Ronnie Lott made them one of the most feared teams in the league. Yet it was the Vikings who controlled the action. Wide receiver Anthony Carter torched the San Francisco defense again and again. The speedy receiver racked up a playoff-record 227 yards on 10 catches. He even ran the ball once for 30 yards.

The Minnesota defense was equally up to the task. Montana couldn't manage much in the face of a fierce pass rush. It got so bad that the legendary quarterback was benched in the third quarter. The younger, faster Steve Young didn't fare much better. Minnesota kept rolling on both sides of the ball. The star-studded 49ers were dismantled. The Vikings advanced with a 36–24 victory, their second major upset in a row.

46

The Vikings' total margin of victory in the wins over the Saints and 49ers.

- Minnesota outscored them 80–34.
- Oddsmakers had listed the 49ers as 11-point favorites in the game.
- The Vikings' run ended in the NFC Championship Game.

THINK ABOUT IT

San Francisco coach Bill Walsh yanked Joe Montana from the game in the third quarter. Walsh reasoned that Steve Young would be better equipped to deal with a wet field and relentless Minnesota pass rush. Montana appeared angry at the decision. How badly would a superstar player have to play to warrant being benched in a playoff game? Did Walsh pull Montana too soon?

BACKUP LEADS GIANTS TO TITLE

The New York Giants started the 1990 season looking like the team to beat. New York won its first 10 games. Then disaster struck. The Giants lost three of the next four. Star quarterback Phil Simms was lost to injury. Yet the Giants kept pushing on with career backup Jeff Hostetler. A power running game and the league's top-rated defense helped them reach the Super Bowl. There, they met the mighty Buffalo Bills, owners of the league's top offense.

With a relative unknown at quarterback, the Giants were 6.5-point underdogs. Few thought they could contain quarterback Jim Kelly and Buffalo's famous no-huddle offense. Yet with eight seconds to go, the Giants held a 20–19 lead. The Bills, however, had the ball at New York's 29-yard line.

New York Giants wide receiver Stephen Baker makes a catch for a touchdown in Super Bowl XXV.

10

Pro Bowlers on Buffalo's 1990 team. The Giants had seven.

- The Giants won the time-of-possession battle 40:33 to 19:37.
- Scott Norwood's kick is known simply as "Wide Right" in Buffalo

Bills kicker Scott Norwood trotted onto the field. It all came down to one field goal attempt.

Snap. Hold. Kick! Everyone watched the ball sail through the air. It drifted farther and farther right,

A DYNASTY THAT WASN'T

Starting with the 1990 season, the Bills won four straight AFC championships. Over that stretch, they went 49–15 in the regular season. Yet the Bills lost all four Super Bowls. The loss to the Giants—especially Scott Norwood's missed kick—still symbolizes the frustration many Bills fans feel at the four straight Super Bowl defeats.

just barely outside the upright. Wide right! No good! The Giants stormed the field. Even with a backup quarterback, they were the champs.

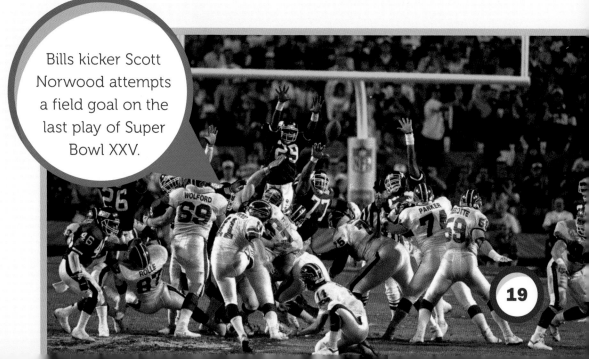

Bills kicker Scott Norwood attempts a field goal on the last play of Super Bowl XXV.

NEW KID ON THE BLOCK PULLS A SHOCKER

Nobody had expected the Jacksonville Jaguars to make the playoffs after the 1996 season. The team was in just its second year. Yet the Jaguars earned a surprising playoff berth after going 9–7. Their amazing run was made even more shocking when they beat the Buffalo Bills in the opening round. Most experts believed that's where they story would end. The Jags traveled to Denver to face the Broncos in the divisional round. Denver had the AFC's best record. It was a 12.5-point favorite.

The Broncos imposed their will early on. The offense, led by legendary quarterback John Elway, jumped out to a 12–0 lead. An interception by the Broncos in the second quarter appeared to have them in complete control. But officials called the play back for pass interference. Replays showed that the call was questionable at best.

The Jags took advantage. They stunned the Denver crowd by scoring 23 straight points. Elway and the Broncos attempted a comeback.

30–27
Final score of each of the Jaguars' 1996 playoff victories.

- Jacksonville made the AFC title game despite being outscored 335–325 during the regular season.
- The NFL's other second-year team, the Carolina Panthers, advanced to the NFC Championship Game that season as well.

But Jacksonville quarterback Mark Brunell put that to an end. He hit receiver Jimmy Smith with a 16-yard touchdown strike in the fourth quarter. Final score: Jacksonville 30, Denver 27. The second-year team was headed to the AFC Championship Game.

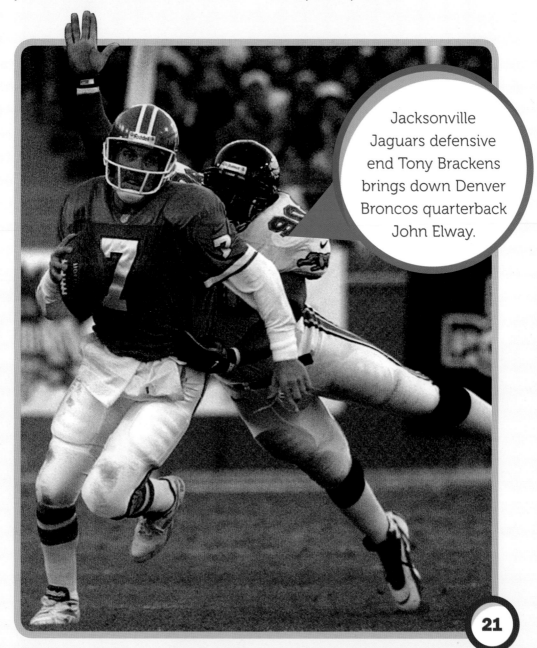

Jacksonville Jaguars defensive end Tony Brackens brings down Denver Broncos quarterback John Elway.

10

THE BRONCOS BITE BACK

The Green Bay Packers came into Super Bowl XXXII in January 1998 looking ready to defend their championship. They had a star quarterback in Brett Favre. Plus they also had a powerful running game and a great defense. Oddsmakers listed Green Bay as overwhelming 11-point favorites over the Denver Broncos. After their shocking playoff loss the year before, however, the Broncos players said they were extra motivated. And it showed.

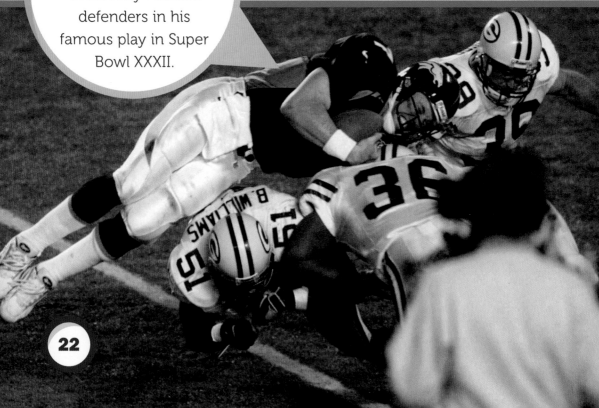

Denver Broncos quarterback John Elway is flipped by Green Bay Packers defenders in his famous play in Super Bowl XXXII.

The game was tied 17–17 in the third quarter. Denver was driving. Quarterback John Elway took the snap and scanned the field. Nobody was open. So Elway tucked the ball and ran up the middle. He could have slid to avoid a hit. But he wanted every yard he could get. Near the 6-yard line, Green Bay safety LeRoy Butler met Elway. Butler went for a big hit. Elway tried to jump over the safety. The 37-year-old quarterback spun through the air and crashed hard to the turf. Denver fans held their breath, but Elway popped right back up. A few plays later, running back Terrell Davis punched the ball in for the go-ahead score.

The Packers eventually tied the score at 24. But Davis punched in the game-winning touchdown with 1:47 left. When Denver stopped the Packers' final drive, the Broncos were finally the champions after four Super Bowl losses.

8

Yards gained on John Elway's famous third-quarter run in Super Bowl XXXII.

- Terrell Davis rushed for 157 yards and three touchdowns. He was named Super Bowl MVP.
- The Broncos won the Super Bowl again the next season. This time they beat the Atlanta Falcons 34–19.

THINK ABOUT IT

With 1:47 to go and the game tied 24–24, the Packers faced a nearly impossible situation. Denver had the ball on Green Bay's 1-yard line. The Broncos could try to score a touchdown. If they failed, they would still have an opportunity to kick a short field goal. So Packers coach Mike Holmgren told his players to let Denver score. That way Green Bay got the ball back with time to score. The Packers didn't score. But was it the right decision? Or should Green Bay have tried for a strip to force a fumble?

THE LEGEND OF TOM BRADY IS BORN

Kurt Warner was unknown to most fans when the 1999 season began. When it ended, the St. Louis Rams' quarterback was a superstar and Super Bowl champion. Two years later, Tom Brady did the same thing. And the New England Patriots' quarterback capped it off with a win over Warner and the Rams in Super Bowl XXXVI.

Despite the Patriots' strong season, the Rams were 14-point favorites. The game started with the Rams'

New England Patriots quarterback Tom Brady looks to make a play in Super Bowl XXXVI.

offensive players being introduced one by one. Then, when it was New England's turn, Brady and the Patriots all ran out onto the field together.

It made a statement and set the tone. Through three quarters, the Patriots defense shut down the league's most electric offense. New England took a 17–3 lead into the fourth quarter. That's when Warner and the Rams finally came to life. With 1:30 remaining, he threw a touchdown pass to tie the game.

Brady had little time and no timeouts. Broadcaster and former coach John Madden said that the Patriots should play for overtime. But that's not what New England coach Bill Belichick had in mind. Brady went out and completed five out of seven passes. With only seconds to play, Brady spiked the ball into the ground to stop the clock. Kicker Adam Vinatieri came out and booted a 48-yard field goal. Game over! The Patriots won 20–17.

Patriots kicker Adam Vinatieri kicks the game-winning field goal in Super Bowl XXXVI.

145
Total passing yards for Tom Brady in the game.

- Despite the low passing yards, Brady was still selected Super Bowl MVP.
- The Patriots became the first team to win the Super Bowl with a score on the final play.
- New England became a dynasty when it won two more Super Bowls in the next three years.

PATRIOTS FALL SHORT OF PERFECTION

Eighteen wins. Zero losses. Tom Brady and the New England Patriots entered Super Bowl XLII in February 2008 looking unbeatable. To many fans and experts, beating the wild-card New York Giants in the Super Bowl was a given. The Patriots were favored to win by a whopping 12.5 points.

The Giants had other ideas. They took the opening kickoff. Then they marched on a drive that lasted 9 minutes, 59 seconds. The longest drive in Super Bowl history ended with a field goal. And it set the tone for the game. The Giants used a fierce pass rush to slow down the powerful New England offense. For three quarters, defense ruled. The Patriots clung to a 7–3 lead entering the fourth.

New York then took the lead. Quarterback Eli Manning found little-used wide receiver David Tyree in the end zone.

The Giants were up 10–7. But Brady responded. With just 2:42 to go, he zipped a touchdown pass to Randy Moss.

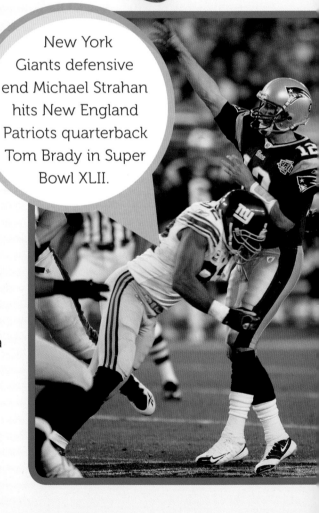

New York Giants defensive end Michael Strahan hits New England Patriots quarterback Tom Brady in Super Bowl XLII.

18–0

The Patriots' record entering the game.

- The 1972 Miami Dolphins remained the only team to go undefeated and win a Super Bowl.
- David Tyree made just five catches for 39 yards all season and playoffs.

That set up one of the most epic drives in Super Bowl history. The key play came on third-and-five near midfield. Manning dropped back to pass. The Patriots defense swarmed. Somehow, Manning slipped away. He heaved the ball down the field. Tyree leaped over his defender. He snagged the ball with one hand and pinned it against his helmet for the catch. A few plays later, Manning hooked up with receiver Plaxico Burress. 17–14 Giants! Thirty-five seconds later, one of the biggest upsets in Super Bowl history was in the books. New England's hopes of perfection were dashed.

REMATCH

The Giants and Patriots met again in the big game after the 2011 season. Once again, the Patriots were favored to win the title (this time by just three points). And once again, Eli Manning and the Giants spoiled their party. New York running back Ahmad Bradshaw scored on a 6-yard run with just over a minute to play. That gave the Giants a 21–17 victory.

David Tyree makes a catch in the fourth quarter to keep the Giants alive in Super Bowl XLII.

FUN FACTS AND STORIES

- After the Browns trounced the Eagles in their first NFL game in 1950, some Eagles complained that all Cleveland did was pass the ball. Cleveland coach Paul Brown took notice. When the teams met again in Week 12, the Browns didn't throw a single pass. They won again, 13–7.

- Denver tight end Shannon Sharpe was crushed after the Jaguars beat the Broncos in the 1996 playoffs. A dejected Sharpe told reporters, "I'm just going to go home, sit on my couch, and probably cry."

- The Patriots' big win in Super Bowl XXXVI has become steeped in controversy. Many people, including Rams players, believe the Patriots cheated. In 2007, New England was disciplined by the NFL for illegally taping an opponent's practice. A story soon surfaced that said the Patriots had done the same to the Rams before the Super Bowl.

- Being a big Super Bowl favorite is no guarantee. Check out the five biggest spreads in Super Bowl history.

Two of them (bolded) were upsets:

Game	Point Spread	Final Score	
Super Bowl XXIX	49ers by 19	49ers 49	Chargers 26
Super Bowl III	**Colts by 19**	**Jets 16**	**Colts 7**
Super Bowl I	Packers by 14	Packers 35	Chiefs 10
Super Bowl XXXI	Packers by 14	Packers 35	Patriots 21
Super Bowl XXXVI	**Rams by 14**	**Patriots 20**	**Rams 17**

GLOSSARY

blitz
A play in which a player who does not normally rush the quarterback does so.

dynasty
A long-lasting period of dominance for a team or player.

favorite
A team expected by most to win.

fluke
An unlikely event that occurs mainly by luck.

merge
The joining of two companies or leagues.

oddsmaker
A person or company that predicts how games will finish; oddsmakers usually set a point spread, predicting how many points the favorite team will win by.

scrambling
When a quarterback runs with the ball, usually to avoid pressure.

spread
A prediction of how wide a margin a team will win by.

underdog
A team expected by most to lose.

wild-card
Playoff spots given to the best teams that did not win their divisions.

FOR MORE INFORMATION

Books

Doeden, Matt. *Football's Greatest Quarterbacks.* North Mankato, MN: Capstone Press, 2012.

Rappoport, Ken. *Biggest Upsets in Sports.* Minneapolis, MN: ABDO Publishing, 2013.

Robinson, Tom. *Today's 12 Hottest NFL Superstars.* North Mankato, MN: Peterson Publishing, 2015.

Websites

NFL Rush
www.nflrush.com

Pro Football Hall of Fame
www.profootballhof.com

Pro Football Reference
www.pro-football-reference.com

Sports Illustrated Kids
www.sikids.com

INDEX

About the Author

Matt Scheff is an artist and author living in Alaska. He enjoys mountain climbing, deep-sea fishing, and curling up with his two Siberian huskies to watch football.

READ MORE FROM 12-STORY LIBRARY

Every 12-Story Library book is available in many formats, including Amazon Kindle and Apple iBooks. For more information, visit your device's store or 12StoryLibrary.com.